Handwriting Practice Paper

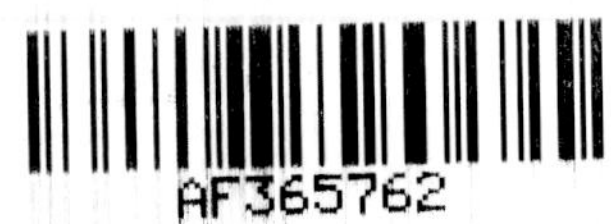

I want to thank You for purchasing This Book. I would be very grateful for taking a moment and leaving feedback. It helps our small business grow and reach more people.